Explore the Bible Yourself

Rick Yohn

NAVPRESS
A MINISTRY OF THE NAVIGATORS
P.O. Box 6000, Colorado Springs, Colorado 80934

The Navigators is an international Christian
organization. Jesus Christ gave His followers
the Great Commission to go and make disciples (Matthew 28:19). The aim of The Navigators is to help fulfill that commission by
multiplying laborers for Christ in every
nation.

NavPress is the publishing ministry of The
Navigators. NavPress publications are tools
to help Christians grow. Although publications alone cannot make disciples or change
lives, they can help believers learn biblical
discipleship, and apply what they learn to
their lives and ministries.

© 1982 by Richard V. Yohn
All rights reserved including
   translation
ISBN 089109**1645**

Fourth printing, 1987

Cover photo: The Image Bank West/Alain
Choisnet, photographer

(Originally published as *Firsthand Joy*.)

Printed in the United States of America

CONTENTS

Dr. Rick Yohn served as pastor of the Evangelical Free Church of Fresno, California for thirteen years. He is currently pastor of the First Evangelical Free Church of Orange, California. His published works include:

Character Growth: Priority for Christian Living
Discover Your Spiritual Gift and Use It
Getting Control of Your Life
God's Answers to Financial Problems
God's Answers to Life's Problems
God's Holy Spirit for Christian Living
Now That I'm a Disciple
What Every Christian Should Know about God
Overcoming

DISCOVER THE BIBLE
YOURSELF

ONE OF THE GREATEST experiences of life is the exciting *firsthand* study of the Scriptures.

Throughout my first nineteen years of life I had been taught Scripture by others. I assumed that original Bible study was a privilege limited to preachers and Bible scholars. This assumption continued after the Lord called me into professional ministry, as my instructors in Bible college and seminary offered us deeper understanding of Scripture.

But during my last year of seminary I inhaled a breath of refreshing air. In his course entitled "Analysis of Bible Books," Dr. Howard Hendricks not only demonstrated how to do original Bible study, but also encouraged us to share those same principles with others who wanted to discover truth for themselves.

Having now taught these principles myself over the years, I am convinced that firsthand Bible study is not the privilege of a few, but the responsibility of all.

The apostle John wrote that "you do not need anyone to teach you" because of the anointing we receive from God, and that "his anointing teaches you about all things" (1 John 2:27).

John was referring to God's Holy Spirit who dwells in us. You can learn from him. You need only to walk in fellowship with him and study his word, using a practical method of personal Bible study.

A note of caution: Don't conclude from the passage in 1 John that gifted Bible teachers are unnecessary. God equipped teachers for us so that the body of Christ might grow in maturity. Teachers are necessary. But you don't have to depend on them for understanding Scripture. You have the ability yourself to grasp biblical truth.

You will be wise to check your interpretation of Scripture periodically with those who are familiar with the original languages (Greek and Hebrew). But remember, the Bible was written for *you* to read and study.

This book offers a tried and proven method of original Bible study, for which the principles have existed for years. This method is sometimes referred to as the "inductive" approach to Bible study, or the "scientific" approach. I like Oletta Wald's term: "The Joy of Discovery."

If you plan to use this book in a group or class, each person should prepare by reading the chapter and doing the exercises ahead of time. The group's discussion when you meet together should center around what each person has discovered in these exercises.

I trust that your adventure in personal Bible study will be an exhilarating experience as new truths emerge from the pages of Scripture. So go to it! Discover the Bible for yourself.

Oh, how I love your law!
I meditate on it all day long.
PSALM 119:97

YOUR GOALS

1

TO GO ON A TRIP you can either follow a highway wherever it goes, or first determine where you want to go and then choose the roads that will take you there.

Many people follow the first approach as they study the Bible. They open the Scriptures in scattered places, hoping to arrive at interesting discoveries. But they often lose interest before finding anything.

Others decide first where they want to go in Scripture, and then choose a method to help them achieve their goal most efficiently.

Learning about inductive Bible study is one of the best ways to help you know what to seek in Scripture and how to find it.

WHAT IS INDUCTIVE BIBLE STUDY?

Inductive reasoning, or induction, means taking a number of facts and drawing a logical conclusion from those facts.

This can perhaps be more easily understood by comparing *induction* with *deduction*:

> *Induction* means first examining various facts and then drawing a logical conclusion from them.

Deduction means starting with a statement or idea, and then finding various facts which prove that the statement or idea is true.

We can illustrate these two approaches in this way:

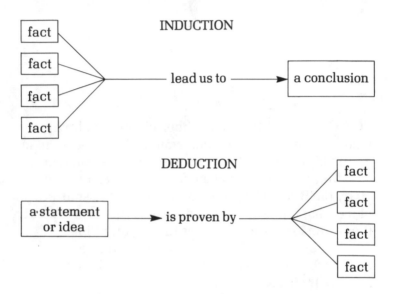

Here's an example of how these two approaches can be applied in Bible study:

Let's say you decide to carefully read and study with an open mind the Gospel of John. As you do so, writing down your discoveries as you go, you notice that many times in this book Jesus claims to be God or makes statements implying that he is God. He also says that he must be obeyed by those who follow him.

You notice also that various people who observed and knew Jesus—including Andrew, Philip, Nathanael, John the Baptist, and Thomas—call him such names as "Messiah," "the Son of God," "the Lamb of God," and "my Lord and my God." These men and other witnesses revered Jesus and worshiped him.

You also see in John's Gospel that Jesus accomplished various miracles—most notably his resurrection from the dead—which vividly demonstrate his claims about himself.

By using inductive reasoning, you conclude from all these facts in the Gospel of John that Jesus Christ is God, and should be acknowledged and obeyed as the Lord of your life. You have arrived at this conclusion on your own by *inductive* Bible study—observing the facts in a portion of Scripture and summarizing a general truth which you discovered in these facts.

In *deductive* reasoning, on the other hand, we start with a statement which we want to prove from evidence in the Bible. Our statement is "Jesus Christ is God and should be acknowledged as our Lord."

To prove this is true, we can use the facts given above from John's Gospel, and also such passages as Peter's statement of faith in Matthew 16:16, Paul's teaching on the supremacy of Christ in Colossians 1:15-20, and the miracle of Jesus walking on water in Matthew 14:25. With this evidence we become convinced that our original statement is true.

In *inductive* Bible study, which is what this book is about, you first look for facts, and then draw your own conclusions based on these facts.

THREE IMPORTANT QUESTIONS

The inductive method asks three vital questions:
1. What do I see? (observation)
2. What does it mean? (interpretation)
3. How does it apply to me? (application)

As you read your Bible with these questions in mind, you fulfill Paul's exhortation to Timothy to be a workman "who correctly handles the word of truth" (2 Timothy 2:15).

What do I see? Learn to go beyond glancing at Scripture, and aim for clear recognition of what God has revealed.

What does it mean? Interpretation is your attempt to discover what the passage you're studying actually means. What did the passage mean to the people who heard these words for the very first time? That is interpretation.

How does it apply to me? To say, "I understand" is good. But to continue with, "Therefore I will obey" is far more important.

Observation, accurate interpretation, and practical application—these are your primary goals as you open the Scriptures for inductive study.

***

Observation means taking thorough, careful notice. It means concentrated looking and thinking.

1. Read Acts 1:8 to see how many *observations* you can make from this verse.
   For example:
   a. The verse begins with the word *but*, showing that the statement to follow is contrasted with what has been said earlier.
   b. A specific event is mentioned as the point at which the disciples would receive power.
   c. This specific event is the Holy Spirit coming upon them.

   What other observations do you see? List as many here as you can:

   _____

   _____

   _____

   _____

_____

_____

_____

_____

_____

_____

_____

_____

_____

_____

2. Now read John 3:16, and try to list *ten* observations you find in this passage.

_____

_____

_____

_____

_____

_____

_____

_____

_____

_____

Group discussion: Share together all your observations from Acts 1:8 and John 3:16, and count them up to see how many different ones the group as a whole discovered for each verse.

KEY WORDS

One way of helping you observe closely the passage you're studying is to look for key words. They are often words which are repeated frequently.

***

1. Read 1 John 4:7-21. What important word is used repeatedly in this passage?

   _____

   How many times is it used?

   _____

2. Now read each of the following passages, and list the important word which is repeated in each one.

   Luke 9:57-62 _____

   _____

   1 Corinthians 6:12-20 _____

   _____

   1 Timothy 6:17-19 _____

   _____

14

Group discussion: How does identifying the key words in these passages from Luke, 1 Corinthians, and 1 Timothy help you better understand the meaning of the passages?

In some passages you may conclude that a certain word or phrase is key even though it is not repeated. For example, in Psalm 1:1-3 you may conclude that the key word is *meditates.*

> Blessed is the man
>> who does not walk in the counsel of the wicked
> or stand in the way of sinners
>> or sit in the seat of mockers.
> But his delight is in the law of the Lord,
>> and on his law he meditates day and night.
> He is like a tree planted by streams of water,
>> which yields its fruit in season
> and whose leaf does not wither.
>> Whatever he does prospers.

CAUSE-AND-EFFECT STATEMENTS

Something else to watch for are cause-and-effect statements. Simply put, these statements say, "If you do *this*, then *that* will happen." If you plant a grain of corn (the cause), then a corn plant will sprout up (the effect). If you receive Christ into your life (the cause), you will become a child of God (the effect).

You can identify many statements of cause-and-effect relationships in Scripture because they begin with words such as *if, because,* and *since.* For example, in Romans 5:1, the first part of the verse is the cause: "Therefore, since we have been justified through faith"—and the rest of the sentence is the effect: "We have peace with God through our Lord Jesus Christ."

***

1. Read John 15:5. What is the stated cause (beginning with the word *if*)?

   _____

   What is the effect?

   _____

2. In 1 John 1:9, what is the stated cause?

   _____

   What is the effect?

   _____

   _____

3. In 1 John 5:14, what is the stated cause?

   _____

   And what is the effect?

   _____

Group discussion: After identifying their cause-and-effect statements, what principles can you draw from John 15:5, 1 John 1:9, and 1 John 5:14?

COMMANDS
AND LINKS

COMMANDS

When someone makes a command, he gives an instruc-
tion or an order that he expects to be carried out. We
can think of it as a requirement or a rule. Scripture
contains many direct commands. For example, look at
these words Jesus spoke in Matthew 5:14-16.

> You are the light of the world. A city on a hill cannot be
> hidden. Neither do people light a lamp and put it under
> a bowl. Instead they put it on its stand, and it gives light
> to everyone in the house. In the same way, let your light
> shine before men, that they may see your good deeds
> and praise your Father in heaven.

This passage, which teaches how Christ's disciples
are the light of the world, contains one direct command: *Let your light shine before men.*

***

List here and on page 18 the commands in Romans
12:9-13.

_____

_____

_____

_____

_____

_____

_____

_____

_____

Select one of these commands, and tell how you could put it into practice in your life more effectively.

_____

_____

_____

_____

Group discussion: How are all these commands in Romans 12:9-13 related to each other?

LINKING WORDS

To cement various phrases and sentences together in Scripture in the right way, various connecting words are used. These little words often play an important role in giving meaning and understanding to a passage.

The important word *but* is used to show contrast. For example, Paul makes this statement in Titus 1:16 about certain people who were spreading false teachings: "They claim to know God, *but* by their actions they deny him."

To emphasize a purpose, the phrases *so that* or *in order that* are often used: "We know also that the Son of God has come and has given us understanding, *so that* we may know him who is true" (1 John 5:20).

Words such as *for* and *because* introduce reasons, as in Psalm 136:1: "Give thanks to the Lord, *for* he is good."

The word *if* introduces a condition: "*If* we walk in the light, as he is in the light, we have fellowship with one another, and the blood of Jesus, his Son, purifies us from every sin" (1 John 1:7).

There are many other linking words as well, most of which you use often in your own speech.

***

1. Read Acts 1:6-8, and look for the importance of the connecting word *but* at the beginning of verse 8. What were the disciples looking for?

   _____

   _____

   What, instead, did Jesus say they would receive?

   _____

2. Find the linking word used most often in Acts 9:23-28. What is it?

   _____

3. Read Ephesians 4:11-16. List here the major linking words in this passage:

   _____

   _____

   _____

   _____

Group discussion: After identifying the linking words in Ephesians 4:11-16, tell what each of them means and how important each one is in this passage.

4

ASKING SIMPLE QUESTIONS such as those suggested below can be your most important tool for making exciting discoveries in observation.

Who?

> Who is this passage talking about?
>
> Who are these words addressed to?
>
> Who wrote or spoke these words?

What?

> What kind of passage is this? Poetry? Narrative? Direct teaching? Prophetic?
>
> What is the atmosphere of this passage—Calm? Emotionally intense? Fearful? Rejoicing?
>
> What happens in this passage?
>
> What precedes this passage, and what follows it?
>
> What do I learn about God, Jesus Christ, or the Holy Spirit in this passage?
>
> What is God doing in this passage?
>
> What difficult words are here, and what do they mean?
>
> What will happen if I follow this person's example?
>
> What will happen if I obey the command God gives here?
>
> What will happen if I later ignore what I'm learning in this passage?

Where?
> Where does the action in this passage take place?

When?
> When did the action occur?

Why?
> Why did the speaker or writer communicate these words?
>
> Why did God allow this to happen?
>
> Why did certain people respond as they did?
>
> Why did Jesus say what he did?

How?
> How should this passage affect my life?
>
> How would I have handled the situation presented in this passage?
>
> How did God work in someone's life in this passage?
>
> How does this passage relate to other parts of Scripture?

***

Using the questions listed above as a mental springboard, read the following passages and record as many relevant questions for each passage as you can. Make every question begin with the words *who, what, where, when, why,* or *how.*

Romans 12:1-2 _____

_____

_____

_____

_____

_____

_____

_____

_____

_____

_____

_____

_____

_____

John 11:1-6 _____

_____

_____

_____

_____

_____

_____

_____

_____

_____

_____

_____

_____

_____

_____

_____

_____

_____

_____

_____

Exodus 18:13-18 _____

_____

_____

_____

_____

_____

_____

_____

_____

_____

_____

_____

_____

_____

_____

_____

_____

_____

_____

_____

_____

_____

Group discussion: Have each group member select one
of the best questions he has prepared for one of the
three passages (Romans 12:1-2, John 11:1-6, and Exodus 18:13-18). Then discuss together as a group a
possible answer for each of the questions selected.

SHARPENING
YOUR FOCUS

I HOPE THE EXERCISES you already have done have whetted your appetite for more Bible study. Many gratifying discoveries will result from your future efforts.

Let's review what we've learned. We've seen that in inductive Bible study we observe the facts and then draw conclusions based on those facts. This inductive method includes the steps of observation, interpretation, and application.

We've seen also that the step of observation can include these methods:

finding key words
identifying cause-and-effect statements
looking at direct commands
examining linking words
asking questions

Now let's put all five of these tools together.

***

1. Read Matthew 15:10-20. Write on page 26 what you think are the key words in this passage.

_____

_____

_____

What cause-and-effect statements do you see?

_____

_____

_____

_____

_____

_____

What direct commands are given?

_____

_____

_____

_____

_____

How are linking words used?

_____

_____

_____

_____

_____

What questions beginning with *who, what, where, when, why,* or *how* can you ask, and how would you answer these questions?

_____
_____
_____
_____
_____
_____
_____
_____
_____
_____
_____
_____
_____
_____
_____

2. Read Mark 6:45-52. What do you think are the key words here?

_____
_____
_____

What cause-and-effect statements do you see?

_____
_____
_____
_____
_____

What direct commands are given?

_____

_____

_____

_____

_____

_____

How are linking words used?

_____

_____

_____

_____

_____

What questions beginning with *who, what, where, when, why,* or *how* can you ask, and how would you answer these questions?

_____

_____

_____

_____

_____

_____

_____

_____

_____

_____

_____

_____

_____

_____

_____

3. Finally, read 1 Timothy 6:6-10. What are the key words in this passage?

_____

_____

What cause-and-effect statements do you see?

_____

_____

_____

_____

_____

What direct commands are given?

_____

_____

_____

_____

_____

How are linking words used?

_____

_____

_____

_____

_____

What questions beginning with *who, what, where, when, why,* or *how* can you ask, and how would you answer these questions?

Group discussion: Discuss how these tools of observation led each of you to a better understanding and appreciation of the passages from Matthew, Mark, and 1 Timothy.

WHEN A CHILD is just learning to talk, his most common question is often, "What is that?" But later he will more often ask, "What does that mean?" He has grown from merely observing, to wanting to interpret what he observes.

Now that you have learned about observation in Bible study, you are ready to search for meaning. By basing your thoughts on good observation and guidelines for accurate interpretation, your conclusions about what a passage means will be based on solid evidence rather than off-the-cuff opinions.

BASIC PROBLEMS

Why does the Bible seem so hard to understand at times? Why is it so difficult for us to grasp what God is saying?

The Bible contains principles which are as fresh as a morning cup of coffee. As you read and meditate on Scripture, you can sense that God is speaking to you right now.

But the meaning of the Scriptures can also be puzzling because a wide chasm of history separates our day from the time when the Bible was written. Also, the location of events in the Bible—Palestine— is an area which many of us know little about, and one whose political features have changed often since Bible times.

The ancient Middle East culture in which the writers of Scripture lived and wrote included not only the imprint of Hebrew, Greek, and Roman civilizations, but also Assyrian, Babylonian, Egyptian, and Persian influences. We, however, tend naturally to view the Scriptures through the eyes of traditional and contemporary western culture.

For example, most of us probably picture the Last Supper in the way Leonardo da Vinci portrays it in his famous painting, with Jesus and the twelve apostles seated around a long table. We may therefore have difficulty understanding what the Gospel writers meant when they spoke of "reclining" at the table or of one disciple leaning against Jesus. But the table was more probably round or U-shaped, and, following the custom of the times, Jesus and his disciples reclined on couches or pillows around it as they ate and drank.

Another hurdle to our biblical understanding is that the original Scriptures were written in Hebrew and Greek (plus a few portions in Aramaic), languages much different from English. Furthermore, English itself has changed greatly since the first English translation of the Scriptures six hundred years ago.

Especially valuable in helping us overcome all these hurdles are good Bible dictionaries, Bible encyclopedias, and other biblical reference books. You'll find some of these books listed on pages 71-72. Your church library may have many of these, and they are also available in Christian bookstores.

In Bible study you'll also find it helpful to refer to more than one modern English translation of the Scriptures.

***

Using reference books such as a Bible dictionary, Bible encyclopedia, or Bible atlas, answer the following questions.

1. Paul often used in his letters the word *mystery*, as in Ephesians 3:4, where he spoke of "my insight into the mystery of Christ." What does the word *mystery* mean as it is used in the Bible?

   _____

   _____

   _____

   _____

   _____

2. The most frequently mentioned weapon in the Bible is the sword. What were swords like in Bible times?

   _____

   _____

   _____

   _____

3. On his eventful journey to Rome recorded in Acts, Paul and his companions were caught in a storm shortly after sailing from Crete, and were adrift at sea for two weeks until their ship was wrecked just off the island of Malta (Melita). How far is it, approximately, from Crete to Malta?

   _____

Group discussion: Think of other good questions that you can find answers for in biblical reference books, and look up and discuss these together among the group.

YOUR APPROACH
TO INTERPRETATION

7

WHERE DO YOU BEGIN in interpreting Scripture passages? How can you be sure you're handling God's word accurately? What if you develop an error without knowing it? Wouldn't it be better just to leave Bible interpretation to the experts?

Years of Bible study have convinced me that as we use sound principles of interpretation, our conclusions will agree with those made by respected biblical scholars. So don't be afraid to interpret Scripture. Adopt the guidelines presented in these lessons, and make them work for you.

At the same time, realize that published commentaries can be helpful. Use them, but be careful not to depend on them too much instead of doing your own study.

APPROACH SCRIPTURE FROM A NORMAL, LITERAL VIEWPOINT

Read the Bible as you would other literature, accepting the fact that it includes figures of speech.

For example, when Jesus said, "I am the gate" (John 10:9), he was comparing himself with the nature of a gate. A gate opens and closes. It both provides entrance and prohibits entrance. In the same way, Jesus said, "I am the way and the truth and the life. No one comes to the Father except through me" (John 14:6). Jesus is the gateway to God.

On the other hand, realize that a passage should not be "spiritualized" unless the context requires it. There are some who spiritualize the resurrection of Jesus, claiming that he did not physically rise from the dead. But the normal understanding of resurrection in Scripture is a bodily resurrection. When Lazarus was raised from the dead, a body which could be seen and touched walked out of the tomb. Likewise, when Jesus rose from the dead he said to the disciples, "Look at my hands and my feet. It is I myself! Touch me and see; a ghost does not have flesh and bones, as you see I have" (Luke 24:39).

Remember, too, that the Bible was written centuries ago within the context of an Eastern culture. Your job as an interpreter is to recognize the timeless truth that Scripture contains, and to relate it to your life today.

APPROACH SCRIPTURE FROM A CRITICAL VIEWPOINT

The term *critical* raises a red flag to some because it implies criticism of the Bible. But your critical eye should focus not on the Bible, but on your interpretation of it. Every interpretation must be questioned.

It is good to say, "This is what I believe the passage means." But it is more important to say, "This is *why* I believe the passage should be interpreted this way."

Ask yourself, *Does my interpretation agree with what the rest of the Bible teaches?* This will help keep you from going off on some radical tangent.

Also compare your interpretation with what you know has traditionally been taught in the Body of Christ. Your own discoveries in Bible study will be new and richly rewarding to you, but they probably will not be new to the church as a whole. Even contemporary heresies are in reality old heresies dressed up in new language and style.

DANGERS

Many contemporary sects would not exist today if their founders had realized that believing "only we are right" is a sure sign of fallacy. Paul wrote that all members of Christ's body are interdependent. Each one can be helped by the other (see 1 Corinthians 12:12-31). No single person has a corner on the Holy Spirit or his teaching.

Remember this as you investigate Scripture, realizing also that your own educational, religious, and cultural background and your particular personality greatly influence your view of biblical teaching.

Another basic danger to avoid in interpreting Scripture is the belief that a "spiritual" person will always interpret Scripture accurately. Spirituality in this sense has to do with someone's personal and inner relationship with God, and does not necessarily guarantee his ability to interpret the Scriptures accurately.

***

1. In each of the passages on the next page, find a figure of speech which Jesus used to describe himself, and tell what the figure of speech means.

John 6:48-51 _____

_____

_____

_____

_____

John 8:12 _____

_____

_____

_____

_____

John 10:14-18 _____

_____

_____

_____

_____

John 15:1-5 _____

_____

_____

_____

_____

2. Read in John 13:1-5 about an eastern custom Jesus
   followed, and then in John 13:12-17 read his
   teaching about this act. What is the essential
   lesson that verses 14-15 hold for us today?

_____

_____

_____

_____

3. Read Matthew 6:19-24, and focus your thoughts on the statement in verse 24, "You cannot serve both God and Money." What do you think this statement means?

_____

_____

_____

_____

Why do you think it means that?

_____

_____

_____

_____

_____

_____

Group discussion: What other figures of speech do you recall from the Bible? What do they mean?

PROGRESSIVE REVELATION

God has revealed himself to man. He is not hiding.
His revelation of himself comes to us through nature,
through our conscience, through the Bible, and
through Jesus Christ.

This revelation is *progressive* in the sense that
God has revealed himself in various ways over the centuries, and each time he has imparted to us more information about himself.

An example of this can be found in Hebrews 8,
which discusses the covenant God made with Israel at
the time of Moses, and how it relates to the later "new
covenant" prophesied by Jeremiah and fulfilled in
Jesus Christ. Verse 13 concludes, "By calling this covenant 'new,' he has made the first one obsolete; and
what is obsolete and aging will soon disappear."

Because of progressive revelation, the teachings
in the earlier parts of Scripture find fulfillment and
clarification in the later parts of Scripture.

God did not reveal everything about himself at
one time, nor did he tell everything to any one person.
Therefore, in studying a topic in Scripture we must investigate truth from all of Scripture.

***

1. Read Luke 24:44. What conclusion can you make
   from this verse about how the Old Testament
   relates to the life of Christ as recorded in the New
   Testament?

   _____

   _____

   _____

2. As God revealed it to them, what did these New
   Testament writers—Matthew, James, and John—
   record in the following passages about require-
   ments for answered prayer?

   Matthew 7:7 _____

   _____

   _____

   _____

   John 16:24 _____

   _____

   _____

   _____

   James 4:3 _____

   _____

   _____

   _____

   1 John 5:14-15 _____

   _____

   _____

   _____

CONTEXT

Before asking, "What does this passage mean to me," we should ask, "What did the writer of this passage mean when he first wrote it?" Understanding the passage in its context will help us grasp this single, original meaning.

The verse "I can do everything through him who gives me strength" may have a variety of meanings to those who hear the statement by itself. But when reading this verse in context—Philippians 4:10-13— we see that these words of Paul focused on his ability in God's strength to always find contentment regardless of his living conditions. This passage encourages us to know the Lord can strengthen and help us even in times of financial and material need.

Although a passage of Scripture has many applications, it has only one primary meaning. The context of the passage—which includes both the verses that come before and the verses which follow—throw light on what that single meaning is. Many faulty interpretations are the result of taking passages out of the context and giving them a surface meaning.

Several years ago I encountered a communal group whose leader advocated total allegiance to himself alone. Some members of this group told me that their sole allegiance to this leader was justified according to Proverbs 5:15:"Drink water from your own cistern, running water from your own well." They explained that the leader was their cistern and well, and they were obligated to learn from him alone. But this interpretation doesn't agree with the context.

***

Read carefully Proverbs 5:1-20, which serves as the context for Proverbs 5:15. On the basis of what you see in this chapter, what do you believe the writer means by, "Drink water from your own cistern"?

_____

_____

_____

Why do you think this is what he means?

_____

_____

_____

_____

Any passage of Scripture actually has several contexts, as this illustration shows:

Immediate context

Other books in the Bible by the same author

The rest of the book

All of Scripture

All of these contexts can help illuminate the meaning of the passage you are studying. For example, to gain a deeper understanding of what Paul meant by "Love never fails" in 1 Corinthians 13:8, we can look at how the word *love* is used in other verses of the thirteenth chapter, how it is used throughout the book of 1 Corinthians, how it is used in the other twelve letters written by Paul, and finally, how it is used throughout the Old and New Testaments.

Group discussion: In what ways does the New Testament complete and fulfill the Old Testament?

What are examples you know of how a verse could be taken out of context?

9

LET THE PASSAGE SPEAK FOR ITSELF

No one who studies the Bible is totally exempt from im-
posing on a passage his own ideas or ideas learned
from someone else. So you should always attempt to let
the passage speak for itself.

You are probably familiar with the verse, "Do not
be yoked together with unbelievers." Do you interpret
the primary meaning of this command to be prohibiting
marriage between a Christian and a non-Christian? If
not, you are an exception. Most Christians think of
marriage when reading this verse because this is how
it is so often taught.

But if you read the passage in its entirety (2 Corinthians 6:14-18) you will discover that Paul never men-
tions marriage. Relating the verse to marriage is simply one of many *applications* we can make.

Make an effort to extract meaning *from* the text,
rather than reading meaning *into* it.

***

Read carefully 2 Corinthians 6:14-18, then answer the
questions on page 44.

1. **What are the five questions Paul asks in this passage?**

   a. _____

   _____

   _____

   b. _____

   _____

   _____

   c. _____

   _____

   _____

   d. _____

   _____

   _____

   e. _____

   _____

   _____

2. **What would you say is the key word in each question?**

   a. _____

   b. _____

   c. _____

   d. _____

   e. _____

3. **What do you believe is the basic truth or lesson Paul is communicating in this passage?**

   _____

   _____

_____

_____

_____

4. How could this basic truth be applied in these areas of life:

Dating? _____

_____

_____

_____

_____

Marriage? _____

_____

_____

_____

Business? _____

_____

_____

_____

_____

COMPARE SCRIPTURE WITH SCRIPTURE

Many Bibles have cross-references as an excellent built-in tool for better interpretation. Learn to make use of these references, for they direct you to other passages that will shed light on the one you are studying. (You can also find cross-references in a concordance, a topical Bible, or other reference books.)

The Bible is its own best interpreter, so compare Scripture with Scripture.

* * *

1. In Philippians 3:2, Paul told the believers to "watch out for those dogs," and he identified these "dogs" as being "men who do evil, those mutilators of the flesh."

   The term *dogs* is used also in the passages listed below. Look up each one, and discover from the passage what kind of people the writer or speaker is referring to when he calls them "dogs."

   Psalm 22:16 and 22:20 _____

   _____

   _____

   _____

   Matthew 7:6 _____

   _____

   _____

   _____

   Revelation 22:14-15 _____

   _____

   _____

   _____

   How do these passages help you understand what Paul meant in Philippians 3:2?

   _____

   _____

   _____

   _____

2. Genesis 22 records how God tested Abraham by requiring that he sacrifice his son Isaac as a burnt offering. Abraham took Isaac to a mountain without saying what God had asked him to do.

    As Abraham came close to the place for sacrifice, we read in Genesis 22:5 that he told his servants, "Stay here with the donkey while I and the boy go over there. We will worship and then *we will come back to you.*" What did Abraham mean by this last statement? Did he really expect to return with Isaac, or was he just trying to keep from causing suspicion among the servants?

    We don't find a direct answer in Genesis, but the cross-reference Hebrews 11:17-19 provides interesting information. Read this passage in Hebrews, and then tell what you think might have been on Abraham's mind as he spoke those words to his servants.

    _____

    _____

    _____

    _____

3. Sometimes a passage in the Bible provides its own specific interpretation. An example is Christ's parable of the sower in Matthew 13. Verses 3-9 include the parable as Jesus spoke it to the crowds, and verses 18-23 contain the explanation of the parable which Jesus gave his disciples. Read both the parable and the explanation, and then identify what the symbols below and on page 48 stand for:

    The seed _____

    _____

    The birds _____

    _____

The sun _____

_____

The thorns _____

_____

The good soil _____

_____

_____

INTERPRETATION PRINCIPLES: A SUMMARY

The principles of interpretation presented in chapters seven, eight, and nine are summarized here:

- Interpret the Bible from a normal, literal view-point.
- Use a critical approach; question every inter-pretation.
- Interpret the Bible as progressive revelation.
- Use the context of the passage to discover what the writer originally meant by it. Find the passage's one primary meaning.
- Guard against reading into Scripture what isn't there; let the passage speak for itself.
- Compare Scripture with Scripture; use cross-references.

For additional help in learning how to interpret the Bible, I recommend *Basics of Bible Interpretation* by Bob Smith (Word, Inc., 1978).

Group discussion: Which of these principles of inter-pretation are the most difficult for you to understand and practice? Which are the easiest?

10

GOD HAS SPOKEN to us, and he expects us to respond. He wants us to apply personally the truths we observe and interpret in the Scriptures.

In this way we heed the warning of James 1:22: "Do not merely listen to the word, and so deceive yourselves. *Do what it says.*"

In application we ask, "What does this truth mean for me?" Application means putting truth to *work.*

For example, in studying what the Scriptures say about contentment, you can study verses such as these:

I have learned to be content whatever the circumstances. (Philippians 4:12)

Godliness with contentment is great gain. For we brought nothing into the world, and we can take nothing out of it. But if we have food and clothing, we will be content with that. (1 Timothy 6:6-8)

Keep your lives free from the love of money and be content with what you have, because God has said, "Never will I leave you; never will I forsake you." (Hebrews 13:5)

Applying these truths to your life could result in any of these steps:

- getting rid of a wrong attitude toward God—such as feeling he's trying to keep you poor, or wants to take all the fun out of your life;
- no longer coveting the possessions of those who own more than you;
- not basing your sense of self-worth on the amount of money you make;
- not allowing difficult circumstances to trap you in negative emotions;
- giving personal relationships a higher priority than your own financial well-being.

Another example: Perhaps as you study some of the biblical teaching on forgiveness, your next-door neighbor comes to your mind. You saw him kick your cat, and you find it difficult to forgive him. But you remember how God in Christ has forgiven you whenever you needed forgiveness.

You become convinced you must forgive your neighbor, and then you think of various ways you could demonstrate that forgiveness. You could chat with your neighbor the next time you see him outside, and break the cold-shoulder routine. You could apologize to him for your cat getting into his flower bed. When he goes on vacation, you could watch his house for him and collect his mail. You could also treat his dog as if it were your own, and stop kicking the fence to make the dog bark.

Can you see the difference between *interpretation* and *application*? Applying the truth of God's word means making it work in your life—sometimes painfully so. Only by application will you grow toward spiritual maturity.

Application should be personal:

What does this passage mean to me?

What dangers do I face if I disobey what God commands in this passage?
What are the benefits for me if I obey this command?

Application must also be practical:

What steps could I take to put this truth into practice?
What will I do today in order to obey what God is teaching me in this passage?

It is not always easy to answer the question *How does this truth apply to my life?* Unless we are primed to receive God's truth into our lives, it may pass by without notice. Then complacency can set in like rigor mortis.

Asking the following questions about a passage you study can help you be receptive to applying the passage personally.

Application Questions

1. How should this truth affect my *attitudes*—what I think about God, other people, my circumstances, and about the way I look at my life in general?
2. How should this truth affect my *knowledge* of God?
3. How should this truth affect my *behavior*?
   What habits should be changed?
   What changes should I make in the way I speak to or about others?
   Does this truth confirm something I am already doing right?
4. How should this truth affect my *relationships* with God and others?
   Do I need to forgive someone?
   Do I need to seek forgiveness myself?
   Should I encourage someone?
   Do I need to rebuke someone?
   Do I need to be more submissive?
   Should I be more dominant?

5. How should this truth affect my *motives* in life? Am I doing the right things but with the wrong motives?
6. How should this truth affect my *values* in life? What is important to me now? What should be important to me?
7. How should this truth affect my *priorities* in life? Who or what really comes first in my life? Who or what should come first?
8. How should this truth affect my *character*? Am I self-centered, or do I demonstrate Christlikeness?

***

Look back over some of the Bible study exercises you did in previous chapters, and select one passage which you would like to apply more deliberately to your life. Then select at least three of the application questions in the list above, and write answers for the questions in the space below.

_____

_____

_____

_____

_____

_____

_____

_____

_____

_____

_____

_____

What practical steps could you take to put this truth
into practice?

What will you do now to obey what God is teaching you
in this passage?

The application chart on the following page is another
tool you can use to help you make God's truth practical. You can use this chart to help you make personal applications from your own personal Bible study,
from sermons and messages you hear, or from your
Sunday school lessons.

Don't be overwhelmed by all the spaces. Each
time you make an application, select only one or two
of the areas. Use the application questions on pages
51-52 to help you pinpoint a step of action you can take
to put God's word to work in your life.

This chart is only an example. You may want to
use your creativity and develop your own chart or
diagram.

Group discussion: What is the difference between interpretation and application? Can application be done
without adequate interpretation?

Areas of life:

Types of application:	Serving God	Devotional life	Family	Job or school	Social life	Finances	Other:
Attitudes							
Knowledge							
Behavior							
Relationships							
Motives							
Values							
Priorities							
Character							
Other:							

REVIEW
AND PRACTICE

11

BY NOW YOU'RE more aware that Bible study and practical application are hard work, but very rewarding. You have a greater appreciation for what Paul meant when he challenged Timothy to be "a workman who does not need to be ashamed and who correctly handles the word of truth" (2 Timothy 2:15).

Let's review the principles and guidelines you've been exposed to in this book.

***

OBSERVATION

1. Name four things to look for in observing a Scripture passage. (See chapters two and three.)

   a. _____

   b. _____

   c. _____

   d. _____

2. What six words are the basic questions of observation? (chapter four)

   _____

INTERPRETATION

3. Certain major problems that often make understanding the Bible difficult can be overcome by
   looking to good biblical reference books. What are
   some of these problems? (chapter six)

   _____

   _____

   _____

   _____

   _____

   _____

4. Summarize the approaches to interpretation
   presented in chapters seven, eight, and nine. (See
   the list on page 48.)

   _____

   _____

   _____

   _____

   _____

   _____

   _____

   _____

   _____

APPLICATION

5. In chapter ten, questions were listed for eight different types of application. Write these eight
   types on the next page.

_____

_____

_____

_____

_____

_____

_____

_____

THE PRINCIPLES AT WORK

6. Read Psalm 23, then write here and on page 58 ten observations on this passage. Your observations can be statements or questions, and can include key words, cause-and-effect statements, commands, and linking words.

    a. _____

    _____

    _____

    _____

    b. _____

    _____

    _____

    _____

    c. _____

    _____

    _____

    _____

d. _____

_____

_____

_____

e. _____

_____

_____

_____

f. _____

_____

_____

_____

g. _____

_____

_____

_____

h. _____

_____

_____

_____

i. _____

_____

_____

_____

j. _____

_____

_____

_____

_____

7. From other portions of Scripture, what else do you know about David's life and his relationship to God that sheds light on the meaning of this psalm?

_____

_____

_____

_____

_____

_____

_____

8. When David wrote this psalm, what do you think was the major truth he was trying to express about God?

_____

_____

_____

_____

9. You may want to use the chart on page 54 to help you make the truth of Psalm 23 more real in your life. What possible steps could you take to put this truth into practice?

_____

_____

_____

_____

_____

_____

10. What will you do now in order to obey what God is
teaching you in Psalm 23?

_____

_____

_____

_____

_____

Group discussion: How did the exercise in this chapter
deepen your understanding of Psalm 23?

Do you feel you now know how to do inductive
Bible study on your own?

THE INDUCTIVE APPROACH to Bible study can be
used to help you understand and apply any passage in
Scripture. Plan now to use this method in a regular
program of personal Bible study in addition to your
daily devotional time of reading and praying.

As you continue in personal study, you'll find
yourself becoming more and more skilled in observing
and interpreting the Scriptures, and God will reward
your diligence in seeking him by helping you apply
what you learn.

Eventually you'll want to do your own inductive
study on entire books of the Bible, perhaps starting
with some of the shorter books in the New Testament
and taking a chapter each week. Meanwhile, here are
some suggested shorter passages for study in the New
Testament that you can choose from:

Overcoming worry—Matthew 6:25-34
Being ready for the end—Matthew 24:36-51
The Great Commission—Matthew 28:16-20
The parable of the sower—Mark 4:1-20
Prayer—Luke 11:1-13
The cost of discipleship—Luke 14:25-35
Jesus, the Word of God—John 1:1-18

The Vine and the branches—John 15:1-17
The world's wickedness—Romans 1:18-32
Righteousness through faith—Romans 3:21-26
Peace with God through Christ—Romans 5:1-11
Death to sin—Romans 6:1-14
The Spirit's control—Romans 8:5-11
Honoring God with our bodies—1 Corinthians 6:12-20
Love—1 Corinthians 13:1-13
Our ministry—2 Corinthians 5:11-21
Freedom in the Spirit—Galatians 5:13-26
Spiritual unity—Ephesians 6:10-18
Humility—Philippians 2:1-11
Christ above all—Colossians 1:15-20
Christ's second coming—1 Thessalonians 4:13-5:11
Work—2 Thessalonians 3:6-13
Perseverance—Hebrews 10:19-39
God's discipline—Hebrews 12:1-13
Faith and deeds—James 2:14-26
Hope—1 Peter 1:3-9
Wives and husbands—1 Peter 3:1-7
Loving others—1 John 3:16-24
New Jerusalem—Revelation 21:1-8

You can use the Bible study outline on the following pages as a guide in the future each time you do Bible study.

Make it your lifelong aim to continue in personal study—and enjoy the results for eternity!

Group discussion: Take one of the suggested New Testament study passages and begin studying it together. Start by making a list of observations.

BIBLE STUDY OUTLINE

Date:

Scripture passage:

OBSERVATIONS

  1. Key words:

  2. Cause-and-effect statements:

  3. Commands:

  4. Linking words:

  5. Questions:

INTERPRETATION

6. Relevant information about history, geography, and culture:

7. Language—are there any words I need to better understand?

8. What is the single primary meaning of this passage?

9. What do I think the original readers understood from this passage?

10. Cross-references:

11. Context—what light does the context shed on my understanding of this passage?

APPLICATION

12. Is there a command I should fulfill?

13. Is there a promise I should claim?

14. Is there a sin I should avoid?

15. Is there an example I should follow?

16. Is there a problem I need to solve?

17. What will I do now to obey what God is teaching me in this passage?

Other questions to ask: In order to better understand this command (or promise or example), what words in this passage do I need to know the meaning of? What are the possible dangers to me if I don't apply this passage to my life? What are the benefits to me if I do apply this passage? What changes in my life will take place?

USING THE BIBLE STUDY OUTLINE—AN EXAMPLE

Date: 11/19

Scripture passage: Hebrews 10:19-39

OBSERVATIONS

1. Key words:

"Let us" "confidence" "faith" "persevere"

2. Cause-and-effect statements:

verses 26-27 — If we deliberately keep on sinning, we can expect only judgment and fire.

verse 38 — If we shrink back from faith, God will not be pleased.

3. Commands:

Let us draw near to God.

Let us hold fast our hope.

Let us consider how to spur others on.

Let us not give up meeting together.

Do not throw away your confidence.

4. Linking words:

"Therefore" (verse 19) "So" (verse 35)

5. Questions:

In what ways can I swerve from my hope (verse 23)?

Am I in any way trampling Christ underfoot (verse 29) by any continued sin?

INTERPRETATION

6. Relevant information about history, geography, and culture:

The book of Hebrews probably was written to Hebrew Christians, perhaps to a small group of them who were capable of being leaders, and who may have been located in Rome.

7. Language—are there any words I need to better understand?

"Most Holy Place" (verse 19)—the dwelling place of God himself.

8. What is the single primary meaning of this passage?

We must never waver in our faith in Christ, because of all that he is. We must never let ourselves be consumed by sin, knowing the dreadful power and holiness of God.

9. What do I think the original readers understood from this passage?

That they should cling to faith in Christ rather than reverting to Judaism or sinful worldliness.

10. Cross-references:

Ephesians 3:12—In Christ "and through faith in him we may approach God with freedom and confidence."

1 Corinthians 13:7—Love "always perseveres."

11. Context—what light does the context shed on my understanding of this passage?

A major theme of Hebrews is that Christ is the eternal, perfect revelation of God, and faith in him brings full and eternal salvation. All this is behind the "therefore" in verse 19.

APPLICATION

12. Is there a command I should fulfill?

"Let us draw near to God"—I need to pray about Phil's confrontation, instead of worrying about it.

13. Is there a promise I should claim?

Christ is our great priest, so I can be confident in coming to God. I can bring all this before him.

14. Is there a sin I should avoid?

To shrink back from faith (verse 38) is not pleasing to God. Do I really believe God is at work in this situation?

15. Is there an example I should follow?

They persevered (32-34) even in the face of suffering. Whatever the cost, I must live out my faith in God.

16. Is there a problem I need to solve?

17. What will I do now to obey what God is teaching me in this passage?

Spend noon hour today praying about verses 24.- 25. How can I spur Phil on to love and good deeds? How can I encourage him?

Other questions to ask: In order to better understand this command (or promise or example), what words in this passage do I need to know the meaning of? What are the possible dangers to me if I don't apply this passage to my life? What are the benefits to me if I do apply this passage? What changes in my life will take place?

I can fully expect to be "richly rewarded" (verse 35) if I confidently persevere in faith in this situation, and in other difficulties I face in the future.

Suggested Reading

BIBLICAL REFERENCE BOOKS

The Zondervan Pictorial Bible Atlas edited by E. M.
    Blaiklock (Zondervan Publishing House, 1969).
Manners and Customs of the Bible by James Freeman
    (Logos International, 1972).
Halley's Bible Handbook by Henry H. Halley (Zonder-
    van Publishing House, 1962).
The New Bible Dictionary (Wm. B. Eerdmans
    Publishing Co., 1962).
Wycliffe Bible Encyclopedia (two volumes) edited by
    Charles F. Pfeiffer (Moody Press, 1975).
The Old Testament Speaks by Samuel J. Schultz
    (Harper and Brothers, 1960).
The Zondervan Pictorial Encyclopedia of the Bible
    edited by Merrill C. Tenney (Zondervan
    Publishing House, 1975).
Introduction to the New Testament by Henry C.
    Thiessen (Wm. B. Eerdmans Publishing Co., 1960).
Archaeology and the New Testament by Merrill F.
    Unger (Zondervan Publishing House, 1962).
Archaeology and the Old Testament by Merrill F.
    Unger (Zondervan Publishing House, 1954).
Unger's Bible Dictionary by Merrill F. Unger (Moody
    Press, 1957).
Unger's Bible Handbook by Merrill F. Unger (Moody
    Press, 1966.)
Manners and Customs of Bible Lands by Fred Wight
    (Moody Press, 1953).
A Survey of Israel's History by Leon Wood (Zondervan
    Publishing House, 1970).

BOOKS ON BIBLE STUDY

Success, Motivation, and the Scriptures by William H.
    Cook (Broadman Press, 1974).
Getting into the Bible by Sandy Dengler (Moody Bible
    Institute, 1979).

Synthetic Bible Studies by James M. Gray (Fleming H. Revell, 1923).

A Layman's Guide to Interpreting the Bible by Walter A. Henrichsen (NavPress and Zondervan Publishing House, 1978).

Enjoy Your Bible by Irving L. Jensen (Moody Press, 1969).

Independent Bible Study by Irving L. Jensen (Moody Press, 1963).

The Layman's Bible Study Notebook by Irving L. Jensen (Harvest House, 1978).

How to Study the Bible edited by John B. Job (InterVarsity Press, 1976).

How to Study the Bible for Yourself by Tim LaHaye (Harvest House, 1976).

Better Bible Study by A. Berkeley Mickelsen and Alvera M. Mickelsen (Gospel Light Publications, 1977).

The Navigator Bible Studies Handbook (NavPress, 1979).

Creative Bible Study by Lawrence O. Richards (Zondervan Publishing House, 1971).

Creative Bible Teaching by Lawrence O. Richards (Moody Press, 1970).

Basics of Bible Interpretation by Bob Smith (Word Books, 1978).

Knowing Scripture by R. C. Sproul (InterVarsity Press, 1973).

Methodical Bible Study by Robert A. Traina (Biblical Seminary in New York, 1957).

Effective Bible Study by Howard F. Vos (Zondervan Publishing House, 1956).

The Joy of Discovery by Oletta Wald (Bible Banner Press, 1956).

The Joy of Teaching Discovery Bible Study by Oletta Wald (Augsburg Publishing House, 1976).

Knock Knock

Jokes for Kids

Uncle Amon

"A good laugh is sunshine in the house."

— William Thackeray

CONTENTS

WHAT IS A JOKE?

joke - something said or done to provoke laughter or cause amusement, as a witticism, a short and amusing anecdote, or a prankish act.

Did you know?

Laughter can have positive physical and mental effects on your body. Laughter can make you feel happy and help create bonds with friends and family.

Jokes come in many forms. It can be a one-liner, question and answer, silly stories, funny movies, and lots more.

Share a laugh with a friend today!

KNOCK KNOCK JOKES FOR KIDS!

Knock knock!

Who's there?

Cows!

Cows who?

Cows go moo not who!

Knock knock!

Who's there?

Cotton!

Cotton who?

Cotton a trap!

Knock knock!

Who's there?

Cod!

Cod who?

Cod red-handed!

Knock knock!

Who's there?

Chuck!

Chuck who?

Chuck in a sandwich for lunch!

Knock knock!

Who's there?

Albert!

Albert who!

Albert you don't know who this is!

Knock knock!

Who's there?

Aldo!

Aldo who?

Aldo anywhere with you!

Knock knock!

Who's there?

Costa!

Costa who?

Costa lot!

Knock knock!

Who's there?

Cook!

Cook who?

Cuckoo yourself, I didn't come here to be insulted!

Knock knock!

Who's there?

Cookie!

Cookie who?

Cookie quit and now I have to make all the food!

Knock knock!

Who's there?

Cole!

Cole who?

Cole as a cucumber!

Knock knock!

Who's there?

Coffin!

Coffin who?

Coffin and spluttering!

Knock knock!

Who's there?

Acid!

Acid who?

Accidently on purpose!

Knock knock!

Who's there?

Comic!

Comic who?

Comic and see me sometime!

Knock knock!

Who's there?

Clark!

Clark who?

Clark your car in the garage!

Knock knock!

Who's there?

Clare!

Clare who?

Clare your throat before you speak!

Knock knock!

Who's there?

A Fred!

A Fred who?

Who's a Fred of the big bad wolf?

Knock knock!

Who's there?

Agatha!

Agatha who?

Agatha headache. Do you have medicine?

Knock knock!

Who's there?

Agent!

Agent who?

Agentle breeze!

Knock knock!

Who's there?

Ahmed!

Ahmed who?

Ahmed a big mistake coming here!

Knock knock!

Who's there?

Aladdin!

Aladdin who?

Aladdin the street wants a word with you!

Knock knock!

Who's there?

Alba!

Alba who?

Alba in the kitchen if you need me!

Knock knock!

Who's there?

Rain!

Rain who?

Rain deer. The same ones that lead Santa's sleigh.

Knock knock!

Who's there?

Callas!

Callas who?

Callas should be removed by a podiatrist!

Knock knock!

Who's there?

It's Sam.

It's Sam who?

It's Sam person that knocked on the door earlier!

Knock knock!

Who's there?

Cain!

Cain who?

Cain you tell? It's me!

Knock knock!

Who's there?

Butch!

Butch who?

Butch your arms around me!

Knock knock!

Who's there?

Albee!

Albee who?

Albee a monkey's uncle!

Knock knock!

Who's there?

Coda!

Coda who?

Coda paint!

Knock knock!

Who's there?

Alec!

Alec who?

Alec-tricity. Isn't that a shock!

Knock knock!

Who's there?

Aleta!

Aleta who?

Aleta from the bill man!

Knock knock!

Who's there?

Aitch!

Aitch who?

Bless you!

Knock knock!

Who's there?

Ear!

Ear who?

Ear you are. I've been looking for you!

Knock knock!

Who's there?

Bunny!

Bunny who?

The bunny thing is that I've forgotten now!

Knock knock!

Who's there?

Cameron!

Cameron who?

Cameron film are needed to take pictures!

Knock knock!

Who's there?

Geno!

Geno who?

Geno any good jokes?

Knock knock!

Who's there?

Cantaloupe!

Cantaloupe who?

Cantaloupe with you tonight!

Knock knock!

Who's there?

Earl!

Earl who?

Earl be glad when you finally open the door!

Knock knock!

Who's there?

Cannelloni!

Cannelloni who?

Cannelloni some money until next week?

Knock knock!

Who's there?

Bruno!

Bruno who?

Bruno more tea for me!

Knock knock!

Who's there?

Bruce!

Bruce who?

I Bruce very easily. Please don't hit me!

Knock knock!

Who's there?

Byron!

Byron who?

Byron some new clothes!

Knock knock!

Who's there?

Jade!

Jade who?

Jade an entire birthday cake this morning!

Knock knock!

Who's there?

Buster!

Buster who?

Buster tire, can I use your phone?

Knock knock!

Who's there?

China!

China who?

China late, isn't it?

Knock knock!

Who's there?

Ten!

Ten who?

Ten to your own business!

Knock knock!

Who's there?

Bush!

Bush who?

Bush your money where your mouth is!

Knock knock!

Who's there?

Two!

Two who?

Two be or not two be? That is the question.

Knock knock!

Who's there?

Burton!

Burton who?

Burton in the hand is worth two in the bush!

Knock knock!

Who's there?

Cherry!

Cherry who?

Cherry oh, see you later!

Knock knock!

Who's there?

Tuna!

Tuna who?

Tuna guitar and it will sound much better!

Knock knock!

Who's there?

Bully!

Bully who?

Bully Jean is not my lover!

Knock knock!

Who's there?

Sarah!

Sarah who?

Sarah other way in?

Knock knock!

Who's there?

Bullet!

Bullet who?

Bullet all the hay and now he's hungry again!

Knock knock!

Who's there!

Bond!

Bond who?

Bond to succeed!

Knock knock!

Who's there?

Candace!

Candace who?

Candace with love!

Knock knock!

Who's there?

Caroline!

Caroline who?

Caroline of rope with you!

Knock knock!

Who's there?

Bjorn!

Bjorn who?

Bjorn with a silver spoon in his mouth!

Knock knock!

Who's there?

Biro!

Biro who?

Biro light of the moon!

Knock knock!

Who's there?

Ada!

Ada who?

A diamond is forever!

Knock knock!

Who's there?

Adair!

Adair who?

Adair once but now I'm bald now!

Knock knock!

Who's there?

Adam!

Adam who?

Adam up and tell me the total!

Knock knock!

Who's there?

Adelia!

Adelia who?

Adelia the cards after you cut the deck!

Knock knock!

Who's there?

Adeline!

Adeline who?

Adeline extra to the letter!

Knock knock!

Who's there?

Adolf!

Adolf who?

Adolf ball hit me in the mouth!

Knock knock!

Who's there?

Burglar!

Burglar who?

Burglars don't knock!

Knock knock!

Who's there?

Adore!

Adore who?

Adore stands between us, open up!

Knock knock!

Who's there?

Banana!

Banana who?

Banana split so ice creamed!

Knock knock!

Who's there?

Abbey!

Abbey who?

Abbey stung me on the nose!

Knock knock!

Who's there?

Aaron!

Aaron who?

Aaron the barber's floor!

Knock knock!

Who's there?

Baby owl!

Baby owl who?

Baby owl see you later!

Knock knock!

Who's there?

Bacon!

Bacon who?

Bacon a cake for your birthday!

Knock knock!

Who's there?

Cindy!

Cindy who?

Cindy next one in please!

Knock knock!

Who's there?

Bach!

Bach who?

Bach to work!

Knock knock!

Who's there?

Cologne!

Cologne who?

Cologne me names won't help!

Knock knock!

Who's there?

Closure!

Closure who?

Closure mouth when you eat!

Knock knock!

Who's there?

Claude!

Claude who?

Claude up by the cat!

Knock knock!

Who's there?

Acis!

Acis who?

Acis spades!

Knock knock!

Who's there?

Curry!

Curry who?

Curry me back home will you?

Knock knock!

Who's there?

Curly!

Curly who?

Curly Q!

Knock knock!

Who's there?

C's!

C's who?

C's the day!

Knock knock!

Who's there?

Crock and dial!

Crock and dial who?

Crock and dial Dundee!

Knock knock!

Who's there?

Crete!

Crete who?

Crete to see you again!

Knock knock!

Who's there?

Razor.

Razor who?

Razor hands, this is a stick-up!

Knock knock!

Who's there?

Edwin!

Edwin who?

Edwin some and you lose some!

Knock knock!

Who's there?

Scold!

Scold who?

Scold out here. Let me in!

Knock knock!

Who's there?

Boise!

Boise who?

Boise ivy!

Knock knock!

Who's there?

Carrie!

Carrie who?

Carrie me home, I'm tired!

Knock knock!

Who's there?

Boiler!

Boiler who?

Boiler egg for 4-5 minutes!

Knock knock!

Who's there?

Bless!

Bless who?

I didn't sneeze!

Knock knock!

Who's there?

Cartoon!

Cartoon who?

Cartoon up just fine. She purrs just like a cat!

Knock knock!

Who's there?

Bun!

Bun who?

Bun-nies make great pets!

Knock knock!

Who's there?

Read!

Read who?

Read between the lines!

Knock knock!

Who's there?

Camilla!

Camilla who?

Camilla minute!

Knock knock!

Who's there?

Gluck!

Gluck who?

Gluck for a spare key for me to have!

Knock knock!

Who's there?

Castro!

Castro who?

Castro bread upon the waters!

Knock knock!

Who's there?

Census!

Census who?

Census lots of presents for Christmas!

Knock knock!

Who's there?

Cassie!

Cassie who?

Cassie the forest for all the trees!

Knock knock!

Who's there?

Beef!

Beef who?

Beef fair now!

Knock knock!

Who's there?

Jess!

Jess who?

Jess the way it is!

Knock knock!

Who's there?

Czech!

Czech who?

Czech before you open the door!

Knock knock!

Who's there?

Brie!

Brie who?

Brie me my supper!

Knock knock!

Who's there?

Egg!

Egg who?

It's eggstremely cold out here. Open up!

Knock knock!

Who's there?

Bridget!

Bridget who?

London Bridget falling down, falling down!

Knock knock!

Who's there?

Bones!

Bones who?

Bones upon a time!

Knock knock!

Who's there?

Shelby!

Shelby who?

Shelby coming around the mountain when she comes!

ABOUT THE AUTHOR

Uncle Amon began his career with a vision. It was to influence and create a positive change in the world through children's books by sharing fun and inspiring stories.

Whether it is an important lesson or just creating laughs, Uncle Amon provides insightful stories that are sure to bring a smile to your face! His unique style and creativity stand out from other children's book authors, because he uses real life experiences to tell a tale of imagination and adventure.

"I always shoot for the moon. And if I miss? I'll land in the stars."
-Uncle Amon

Made in United States
North Haven, CT
29 September 2022

24664738R00028